From the authors:

Newborns don't come with instructions... When the crying starts, loving parents try everything to help their little one. This story follows Mama and Papa Bear as they try to figure out how to cheer up their little Baby Bear. As a new parent, one of the hardest parts of having a little one is not being able to help them right away when you don't know what's wrong. This book is a sweet reminder to handle these times with love and patience.

To my wife and son, the inspiration for this book.
I love you both so much.

The tune is gentle, sweet and low.

But Baby Bear wiggles and tears still flow.

Maybe Baby just has gas?
Kick, kick, kick!
Those legs go fast!
A tiny toot,
but those whimpers last.

Maybe Baby needs a change?
But after Baby is fresh and dry,
Baby Bear still wants to cry.

A little giggle... but it won't last. Then comes crying, loud and fast.

Maybe Baby is too warm?

Papa fans Baby Bear nice and slow.

Still no smiles or relief though.

Maybe Baby is too cold?

Snuggled Baby Bear tucked in tight.

Still not calm... not yet tonight.

Maybe Baby is feeling sick?

Mama checks for a fever -quick!

Baby's temperature seems just fine, and yet...

Baby Bear still whines.

Maybe Baby wants to sway?

So Papa rocks the gentle way.

It starts to work but I hate to say

it seems those tears

are here to stay.

Maybe Grandma and Grandpa Bear know what's wrong?

"Sorry Dear, it's been so long."

Baby Bear sighs all snug and sweet,

then smiles and drifts gently to sleep.

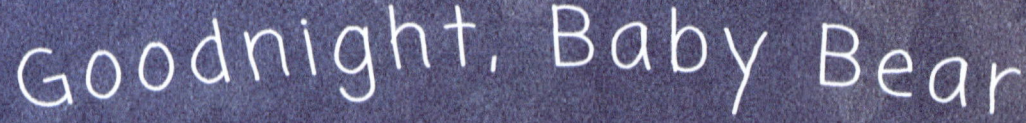

www.ingramcontent.com/pod-product-compliance
Lightning Source LLC
Chambersburg PA
CBHW061405010526
44119CB00011B/268